Forward

The Savvy Consortium was founded to bring together practicing new product development managers to share their best practices. I enthusiastically welcome this as the first publication to come from our members. As practitioners, our emphasis is always on a description of what works. We have always endeavored to create a group formed from a wide range of industries. Even so, our group has tilted to the "durable goods" perspective found in the Lean and "knowledge based" work of Allen Ward, Michael Kennedy, and Jeffrey Liker, et. al. Few durable goods development managers have knowledge of Agile methods, notwithstanding that their software confreres have experiential knowledge and impressive success with Agile.

Steve proposes to change this knowledge gap among durable goods managers of product development. Zielinski, currently a development management professional and program manager with extensive industrial experience, proposes that Lean, Knowledge-based, and Agile methodologies should converge, be learned and adapted. This convergence would leverage product development activity and thereby improve customer expectations, product design, people talent building and process that meet schedules with quality designs and managed risk. He proposes that product developers initiate these three approaches to improve their people and processes, especially at the product development project level.

Zielinski writes for an audience of savvy product development people who are quick to learn, willing to adapt and apply new methods that positively impact their work life.

The author himself has converged these three methodologies in his work and with his development teams who develop software and hardware.

Steve Zielinski represents a generation of managers/authors who are leading the product development and management community to continuously learn and adapt new thinking/practices that impact their design engineering work cultures. We thank him for his willingness to share his insights with the wider product development community.

Jim Jacobs

Co-founder of the Savvy Consortium

The Savvy Consortium was founded to encourage product development teams, engineering managers and directors to share their experiences with others. We are dedicated to helping those interested in converging and adapting Lean, Agile and Knowledge based product development thinking and practices.

http://www.savvyconsortium.com

Introduction

Physicists have for years been in pursuit of a Grand Unification Theory, a model that merges the electromagnetic, weak nuclear, and strong nuclear fields into a single unified field that can be used to predict the behavior of the physical world. This book is an effort to merge the three major new product development methodologies into a coherent whole. Rather than proposing a single universal process of development, we hope that what emerges is a set of universal principles that can be applied and adapted to the unique circumstances of your organization. By exploring the common themes present in Lean, Agile, and Knowledge-based development we hope to create a common framework, as well as an ability to apply the unique strengths of each of these methods.

We'll begin by exploring the changing economics of new product development. Then we'll explore the three dominant philosophies by exploring their histories and principles. We'll end our journey with a proposed framework – something concrete that you can act on and modify according to your unique situation.

Chapter 1 - A World of Changing Economics

"The cat, having sat upon a hot stove lid, will not sit upon a hot stove lid again. But he won't sit upon a cold stove lid, either."

Mark Twain

Engineering education and practice is focused on getting it right the first time. Engineers are taught careful thinking up front is the key to successful and efficient product development. Getting it wrong would be costly in both time and money. This has led us to focus on up front "thought experiments" and created a near reluctance to build anything that has not been carefully thought through. But haven't we also experienced the eye opening reality of prototypes? Haven't we all found the real thing demonstrates essential properties our thought experiments would never have revealed? How do we reconcile these two realities? As it turns out, we don't have to. Reality has changed.

The reality that has changed is the cost of experimentation. It has dropped dramatically. This happened first in the field of software engineering. Computer use costs that were once tracked by the millisecond decreased below the point of being worth tracking. The skeptic's reply to this is "Software is different. I work in a world of physically tangible objects." Fair enough, but the world of the mechanical engineer is undergoing its own transformation. Witness the reality of "additive manufacturing". Consider these stories from Stratasys, one company in the newly competitive 3D printing market. (Note: I have neither affiliation with nor financial stake in

Stratasys. The stories below are just specific examples of a more general trend.)

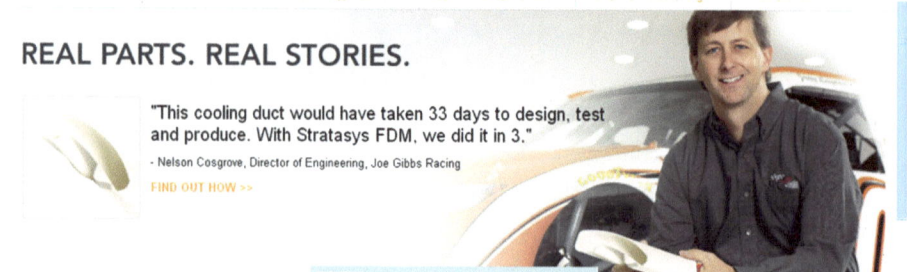

Who wouldn't want a solution 10 times faster?

Experimentation (iteration) can, in many situations, provide faster and more certain results.

One might object to the high cost of investing in the machines required to produce the prototypes above. However, Stratasys and other companies have answered this objection by creating businesses that will make the prototypes for you. Stratasys calls their on demand unit "RedEye On Demand". Consider this story:

> "Wyle's Integrated Science and Engineering Group in Houston helped the National Aeronautics and Space Administration (NASA) prepare the Robonaut 2 (R2) dexterous humanoid robot for launch to the International Space Station (ISS). The estimated time for conventional machining of the parts used for the mockup was **8 months and the cost was $180,000**. Instead, it took only **two weeks and cost $36,000** for Redeye to make all of the parts required for the mockup."

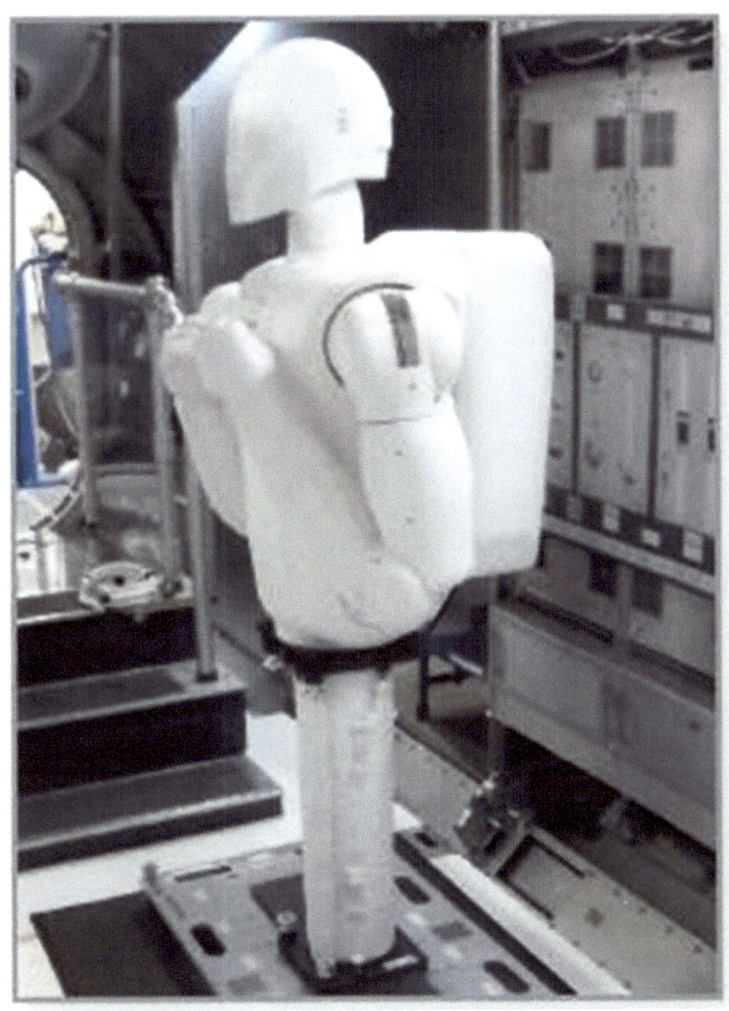

These techniques are also being applied to rather large scale items, such as aircraft landing gear. Consider RedEye On Demand's experience with Messier-Dowty, the world leader in landing gear systems.

"To make the 16-foot-high physical mock-up, Messier-Dowty turned to RedEye for rapid prototyping with its fused deposition modeling (FDM®) process."

"Seeing actual, full-scale parts puts everything in perspective." Lakerdas agrees, "People want to see it, feel it and touch it. You can't do that with a digital mock-up."

The 16-foot tall landing gear mock-up included components measuring up to 18 x 24 x 75 inches (keyboard on lower left corner illustrates scale).

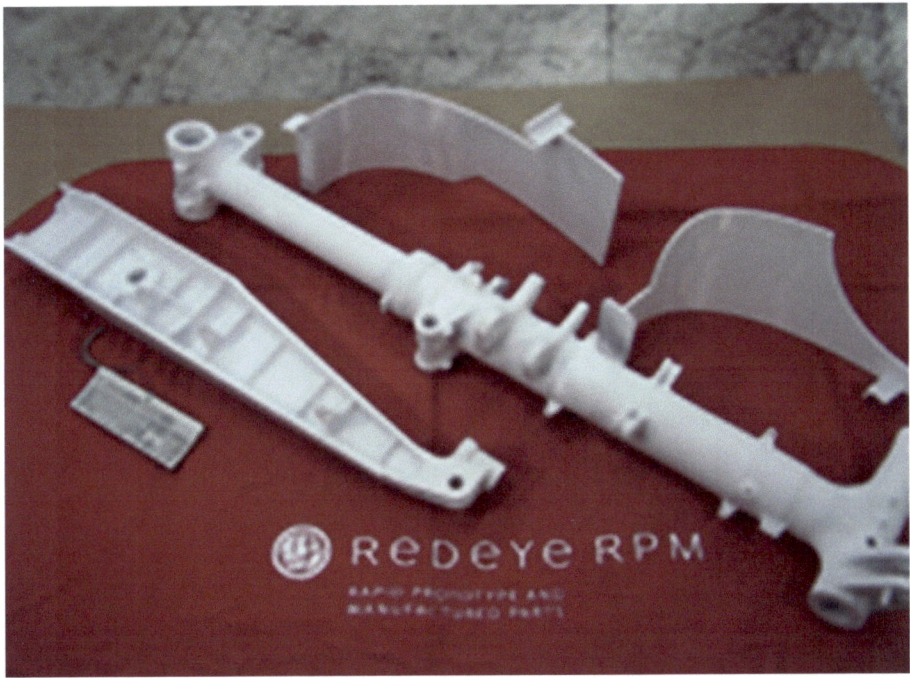

Are your development processes tuned to take advantage of a world where prototype speed and cost have fallen to the levels illustrated above?

There is another level of sophistication available, if you are able to accurately model the problems in your domain. Consider this eye opening example from BMW:

"By studying some early prototype crashes, engineers on the team had learned that in crash after crash, a small section of the B pillar folded." The solution seemed obvious – add metal to the bottom of the pillar. No need to test it. One development team member, however, insisted on verification, pointing out that it would be neither difficult nor expensive to do this via computer simulation. When the program was run, the group was shocked to discover that strengthening the folded area actually decreased crashworthiness... reinforcing the lower part of the B pillar made the part higher up – above the reinforced part – prone to buckling... the solution to the folding-B-pillar problem turned out to be completely counterintuitive: Weaken it rather than reinforce it."

Stefan H Thomke in Experimentation Matters

To sum it up, consider these two quotes from Jim Highsmith:

"When we reduce the cost of experimentation enough, the entire economics of how we do product development changes – it switches from a process based on anticipation (define, design, and build) to one based on adaptation (envision, explore, and adapt)."

"In industry after industry – pharmaceuticals, software, automobiles, integrated circuits, ... the plunging cost of experimentation is signaling a massive switch from anticipatory to adaptive styles of development."

Things have changed and our new product development methods must change with them.

To one degree, or another, the three major new product development methodologies, Lean, Agile, and Knowledge-based, take advantage of this new reality. In the next chapter we will begin our look at their fundamental principles.

Chapter 2 – Lean

"There are three kinds of leaders. Those that tell you what to do. Those that allow you to do what you want. And Lean leaders that come down to the work and help you figure it out."

– John Shook

Of the three new product development methodologies we are going to consider, Lean is probably the most well-known. It had its genesis in the Toyota Production System. Let's take a moment to clarify Lean terminology. First, we must be careful to distinguish two of Toyota's systems:

1. The Toyota Production System

2. The Toyota Product Development System.

Lean principles were first articulated in the context of the manufacturing environment, the Toyota Production System.

In the book Lean Thinking (1996) James P. Womack and Daniel T. Jones distilled five lean principles:
1. Specify the value desired by the customer.
2. Identify the value stream for each product providing that value and challenge all of the wasted steps (generally nine out of ten) currently necessary to provide it.
3. Make the product flow continuously through the remaining value-added steps.
4. Introduce pull between all steps where continuous flow is possible.
5. Manage toward perfection so that the number of steps and the amount of time and information needed to serve the customer continually falls.
A sixth one, Respect for People, is frequently added.

Distilling this down even further we have:

1. Value
2. Value stream
3. Flow
4. Pull
5. Perfection
6. Respect for People

A useful mnemonic for these six principles can be the image of someone fly fishing:

They Value their time in the Stream (Value, Value Stream). They feel the Flow of the stream Pulling at them as they try to achieve the Perfect cast while Respecting others around them.

14

These principles proved so valuable in the manufacturing space there was a desire to apply them to new product development. Let's try to apply these principles to answer a typical question from a product development project:

"How many prototype board iterations should we plan?"

Answer #1: In the interest of reducing waste and minimizing the number of steps, we should plan for only one or two prototype boards. We will seek perfection on the first turn.

Answer #2: Waste is found in the time we spend reviewing schematics, only to realize we still failed some tests when we have an actual board in hand. We should reduce waste by planning four or more prototypes so that a board concept flows smoothly from conception to realization.

Unfortunately, both answers are potentially correct based on the generic lean principles. How would Toyota answer the question? Toyota would answer the question based on the Lean principles embodied in the Toyota Development System (not the Production System).

James M. Morgan and Jeffrey K. Liker, authors of *The Toyota Product Development System, Integrating People, Process and Technology* (2006, Productivity Press), offer the following product development guidelines practiced by Toyota (where an obvious mapping exists to the Lean Principles, it is noted in parenthesis.):

1. Establish customer-defined value to separate value-added from waste. (Value)

2. Front-load the product development process to explore thoroughly alternative solutions while there is maximum design space.

3. Create a level product development process flow. (Flow)

4. Utilize rigorous standardization to reduce variation, and create flexibility and predictable outcomes. (Value Stream)

5. Develop a chief engineer system to integrate development from start to finish. (Pull)

6. Organize to balance functional expertise and cross-functional integration. (Respect for People)

7. Develop towering competence in all engineers. (Perfection)

8. Fully integrate suppliers into the product development system.

9. Build in learning and continuous improvement. (Perfection)

10. Build a culture to support excellence and relentless improvement. (Perfection)

11. Adapt technologies to fit your people and process.

12. Align your organization through simple visual communication.

Reconsidering our question from above, I believe Toyota would favor the creation of additional prototypes based on principles 2 and 9. The additional prototypes are adding value by allowing us to explore the design space and by providing earlier opportunities to learn and adapt.

Finding the opportunity to learn is the driving principle we will encounter throughout the three dominant product development methodologies.

Chapter 3 – Agile

A relentless organizational focus on success makes true experimentation all too rare.

Experimentation Matters, Stefan H Thomke

An Essential Bit of History

Our story for Agile begins in the late 70's or early 80's. The US Department of Defense is experiencing project after project with runaway costs (some things never change). After a bit of investigating they realize the software in these large systems is responsible. The DoD commissions Carnegie-Mellon University in Pittsburgh to help them solve this problem. The bright minds at Carnegie-Mellon form the Software Engineering Institute (SEI) and determine the essential problem with software development is that it is "invisible". There is no clear way to determine how far along a contractor is with the software. That means there is no early warning sign they are off schedule and no way to take corrective actions. How do you make progress on a software project visible? You require documentation! And lots of it. You also insist that contractors finish requirements before beginning design. Design must be finished before you begin coding. In this way you can move in an orderly way from start to finish. This notion of an orderly progression from requirements to design to implementation is actually a tragic accident of misreading. The idea was derived from the figure below found in Winston W. Royce's paper "Managing the Development of Large Software Systems", written in 1970.

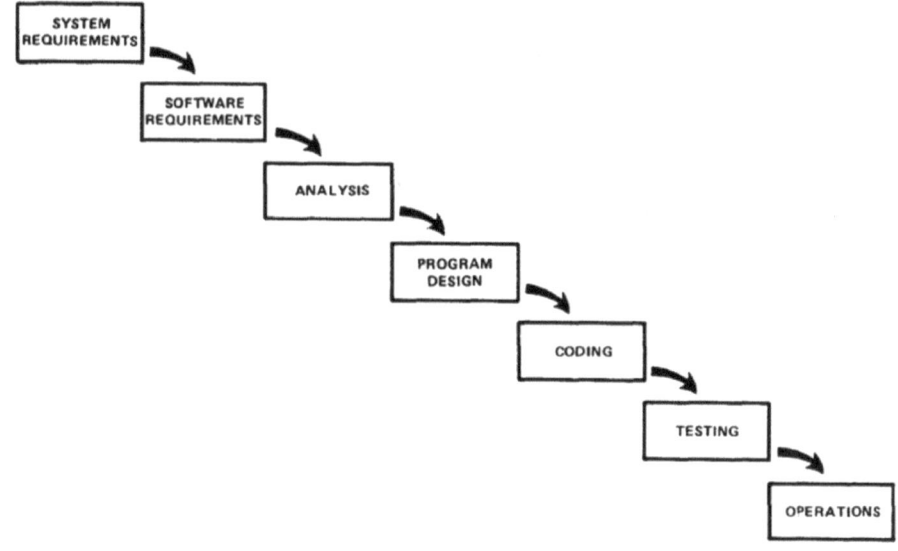

Figure 2. Implementation steps to develop a large computer program for delivery to a customer.

No one seemed to notice that Royce drew the diagram to show the path to failure! He writes:

"… the implementation described above is risky and invites failure."

He then goes on to promote a different process. He recommends to "do it twice" by building a throw-away "pilot model" first to explore novel elements and unknown factors. Unfortunately, the figure above became the model for DOD-STD-2167. It spread from there to Europe. The DoD and many companies spent the 80's and 90's trying to follow this model. Not surprisingly, the rate of project failures did not decline. Companies chased the waterfall model believing that if only their organization would be more rigorous in its implementation of the process they would find success. Indeed, the very notion of waterfall development is very seductive. It appeals to our sense of order. Organizations crave the predictability promised by the approach. Plan carefully and then execute.

18

Our penchant for the waterfall model can be summed up in this way:

> **"there is always a well-known solution to every human problem — neat, plausible, and wrong."[1]**
>
> *H. L. Mencken*

While much of the world chased after the waterfall model, small groups began to explore alternatives. In January 1986 **Hirotaka Takeuchi and Ikujiro Nonaka** wrote a Harvard Business Review article entitled "The New New Product Development Game". In it they wrote:

> In today's fast-paced, fiercely competitive world of commercial new product development, speed and flexibility are essential. Companies are increasingly realizing that the old, sequential approach to developing new products simply won't get the job done. Instead, companies in Japan and the United States are using a holistic method—as in rugby, the ball gets passed within the team as it moves as a unit up the field.

> This holistic approach has six characteristics: built-in instability, self-organizing project teams, overlapping development phases, "multilearning," subtle control, and organizational transfer of learning. The six pieces fit together like a jigsaw puzzle, forming a fast flexible process for new product development. [2]

In 1993 "The New New Product Development Game" was read by a development team at Easel Corporation being led by Jeff Sutherland. This was the first team in the world to practice a specific Agile development method named Scrum (note the rugby reference in the quote above). In 1995 Jeff Sutherland and Ken Schwaber worked to formalize Scrum and presented their paper at OOPSLA'95. Ken and

Jeff had each experienced dramatic success stories with variations of Scrum. Ken was driven to understand why. He sought out friends working at the DuPont Advanced Technology Center in Delaware. The leader of the center was Babatunde Ogunnaike (Tunde), one of the authors of the bible of the process control industry, "Process Dynamics, Modeling and Control".

"Tunde then took me to the realm of empirical process control, a technique used for small batch production when there is more unknown than known, where the complexity is greater than the predictable. He felt that this was more relevant to the field of software development. The churn in our requirements, the complexity of the many technologies, and the use of creative thinking by people made this approach most appropriate. This approach was set up to expect the unexpected through frequent inspection of progress and subsequent adaptation of next steps to optimize output. The basis of it was the container.

A container is a closed space where things can get done, regardless of the overall complexity of the problem. In the case of Scrum, a container is a Sprint, an interaction. We put people with all the skills needed to solve the problem in the container. We put the highest value problems to be solved into the container. Then we protect the container from any outside disturbances while the people attempt to bring the problem to a solution. We control the container by time-boxing the length of time that we allow the problem to be worked on. We let the people select problems of a size that can be brought to fruition during the time-box. At the end of the time-box, we open the container and inspect the results. We then reset the container (adaptation) for the next time-box. By frequently replanning and shifting our work, we are able to optimize value." [3]

This explanation provided the theoretical understanding of why Scrum (Agile) worked and why Waterfall did not.

Others had been discovering these same principles. They gathered at The Lodge at Snowbird ski resort in the Wasatch Mountains of Utah On February 11-13, 2001. From this meeting the Agile Manifesto was born:

Manifesto for Agile Software Development

We are uncovering better ways of developing software by doing it and helping others do it.

Through this work we have come to value:

Individuals and interactions	over	processes and tools
Working software	over	comprehensive documentation
Customer collaboration	over	contract negotiation
Responding to change	over	following a plan

That is, while there is value in the items on the right, we value the items on the left more.

From the above manifesto 12 principles were derived:

The 12 Agile Principles:

1. Our highest priority is to satisfy the customer through early and continuous delivery of valuable software.

2. Welcome changing requirements, even late in development. Agile processes harness change for the customer's competitive advantage.

3. Deliver working software frequently, from a couple of weeks to a couple of months, with a preference to the shorter timescale.

4. Business people and developers must work together daily throughout the project.

5. Build projects around motivated individuals. Give them the environment and support they need, and trust them to get the job done.

6. The most efficient and effective method of conveying information to and within a development team is face-to-face conversation.

7. Working software is the primary measure of progress.

8. Agile processes promote sustainable development. The sponsors, developers, and users should be able to maintain a constant pace indefinitely.

9. Continuous attention to technical excellence and good design enhances agility.

10. Simplicity--the art of maximizing the amount of work not done--is essential.

11. The best architectures, requirements, and designs emerge from self-organizing teams.

12. At regular intervals, the team reflects on how to become more effective, then tunes and adjusts its behavior accordingly.

The 80's and 90's were decades in which a concerted effort was made to turn software engineering into a "true" engineering discipline. The great quest has been to make software yield to the same mathematical rigor found in the physical sciences. It is ironic that the second decade of the 2000's has turned into a quest to make the other engineering disciplines as agile as software.

Agile is all about the iterative and incremental development of working software. It clearly favors the adaptive development approach. Agile arrived at this point by a different route than the mechanical and electrical disciplines. They arrived here by virtue of the changing economics of experimentation. Agile arrived here by virtue of experimentation and the failure of the waterfall method.

Note that once again we find the acceleration has the driving principle of the method. By learning as quickly as possible what works and what doesn't Agile delivers the final product as quickly as possible.

Chapter 4 – Knowledge-based

The only people who achieve much are those who want knowledge so badly that they seek it while the conditions are still unfavorable. Favorable conditions never come."

— C.S. Lewis

I should first disclose that considering knowledge-based development to be an independent development methodology may itself be somewhat controversial. My own belief is that Lean new product development was something of a misunderstanding, or incomplete understanding, of the Toyota Development System. It seems that the "discovery" of the Toyota Production System set off a rush to apply Lean to everything. Indeed, the principles underlying Lean can be applied to new product development, but it was done, at least initially, incorrectly. It seems the first person to understand that Lean was being misapplied in the new product development area was Allen Ward. Ward had independently developed a concept he called set-based concurrent engineering. While at the University of Michigan, Ward teamed up with Jeff Liker to survey auto companies to see if any of them were already using a similar concept. They found that Toyota was using something similar to Ward's concept. Ward visited Japan in 1993. The Toyota Production System was already famous, but no one had yet managed to describe the Development System simply and effectively – including those inside Toyota. Ward began to develop his ideas with Durward Sobek, John Shook, and later Michael Kennedy. In fact, it was Michael Kennedy who proposed the notion that the term "knowledge-based" was a better description than "Lean" for Toyota's new product development system. Certainly, much has been written and many valuable insights have been made when viewing new product development through the lens of Lean. Let's carry on with the notion that knowledge-based is a third philosophy of product development and that it brings with it insights not previously seen.

I think the best summation of knowledge-based development is found in this quote from Michael Kennedy:

> "Product development is not about developing cars, it is about developing knowledge about cars. Great cars will emerge from the interaction." – Michael Kennedy on Toyota [4]

Made in America

Were the principles of Lean and Knowledge-based development, now synonymous with Japanese manufacturers, an American invention? Allen Ward believed the roots of Knowledge-based development are found in the work of the Wright Brothers. Professor Ward passed this understanding on to Michael Kennedy who articulated it this way:

> The Wright Brothers made the observation that all their predecessors and their peers were spending about 5000 hours designing an aircraft and about 5 seconds testing it - which often killed them. Here is a quote from Wilbur. "We thought that if some method could be found by which it would be possible to practice by the hour instead of by the second there would be hope of advancing the solution of a very difficult problem…and without any serious danger." They epitomize the shift in paradigm from "Design then test" to "Test then design" that we so often use to define the Toyota paradigm. The Wright Brothers didn't start with detailed specs; they started by identifying their key knowledge gaps and developing brilliant experimentation techniques to solve them; once solved, then they designed the plane and flew it. To me, it is amazing that most companies today

design their products first in order to find their problems and fix them with loopbacks. Toyota understands the lessons from the Wrights; most companies don't. [5]

The Wright Brothers approach to the development of the airplane was adopted by Japanese aeronautical engineers. These same engineers became the employees of Toyota following World War II. Quite naturally they adapted their aeronautical approach to car design.

To summarize the difference between traditional and knowledge-based development consider the table below [6]:

	Traditional	Toyota
Product Specs	As specific as possible as early as possible	Rough targets to start Details evolve with the project
Design Decisions	Made as early as possible	Delayed as long as possible
Testing	Mostly after design, to fix	Mostly before design, to learn
Project Management	Administrative – to manage process compliance	Technical – to manage knowledge growth into products
Innovation Focus	New product concepts	New product breakthroughs, but mostly subsystem platforms

An important mechanism to adopting knowledge based development is to guide your product development efforts with three questions.

The three questions of knowledge-based development:

1. What decisions do we need to make?

2. What information do we need in order to make those decisions?

3. How will we get that information?

Explicitly asking and answering these questions is surprisingly powerful.

Set-based concurrent engineering (SBCE)

Another major feature of knowledge-based development is the notion of set-based concurrent engineering or set-based design. The name itself frequently leads people to conclude that this means bringing multiple designs through the development process and then very late in the process picking the design with the most desirable qualities. This was not the original intention: " … set-based development is not redundant development. Set-based development is a focused effort of using a set of varied design parameters to create knowledge". This knowledge is frequently gained at the component level. The knowledge gained in previous projects can then be used to match component parts to create a new whole.

In order to do this, a company needs to understand the qualities of the component. Typically, we don't take the time to really understand our components. Instead we ask the most expedient question: "Does it work?" If the answer is "Yes" we plan it into the product and move on.

Consider a story from Harley-Davidson as related in Dantar P. Oosterwal's book "The Lean Machine". Harley had brought a new motorcycle to their premier introduction event in Daytona, Florida. At first everything was going well. Customers were enthusiastic about the performance of the new motorcycle. Shortly, however, the drive belts on the motorcycles began to break during customer test drives. The drive belt connects the motorcycle's transmission to the rear wheel. If the drive belt breaks, the motorcycle can't be driven. These breaking belts were surprising because the belt had actually been used on a previous model with a larger engine. No one expected trouble on a motorcycle with a smaller engine.

Harley had specified the belts needed to withstand 10,000 pounds of pull. The first question was "Did we get a poorly manufactured batch of belts"? They quickly tested belts from the same batch only to discover they all passed the testing. See the figure below.

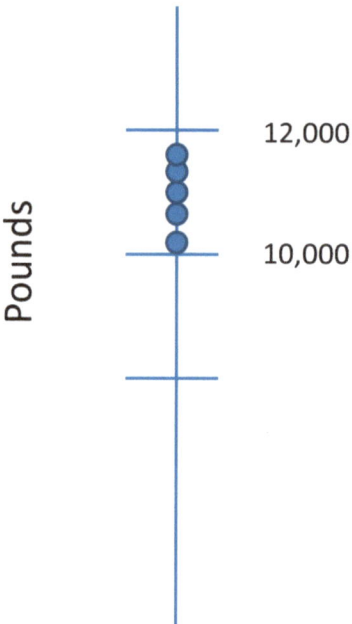

After some additional thinking they decided to ask "Does the belt strength decline with use?" They designed a test fixture to put mileage on the belt and then placed the belt in the load tester.

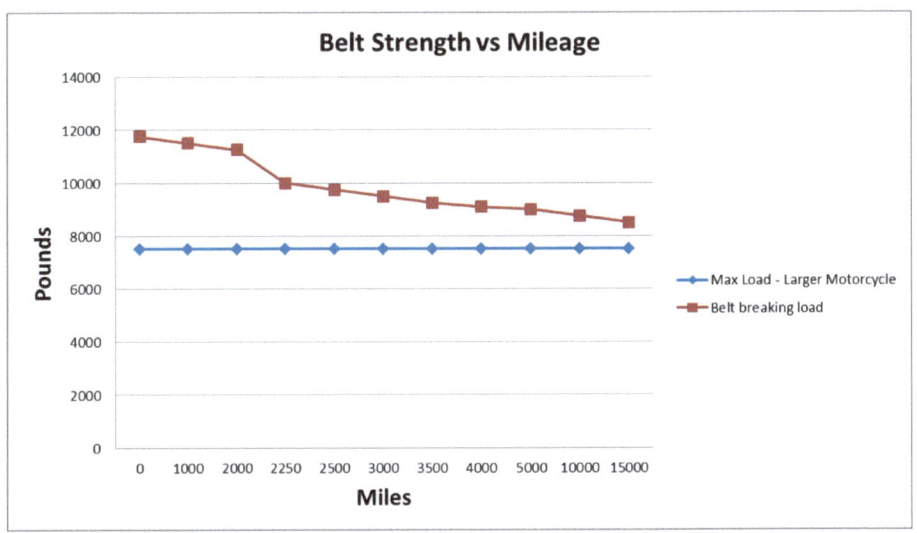

Someone then thought to ask the question "Have we measured the load put on the belt by the smaller motorcycle?"

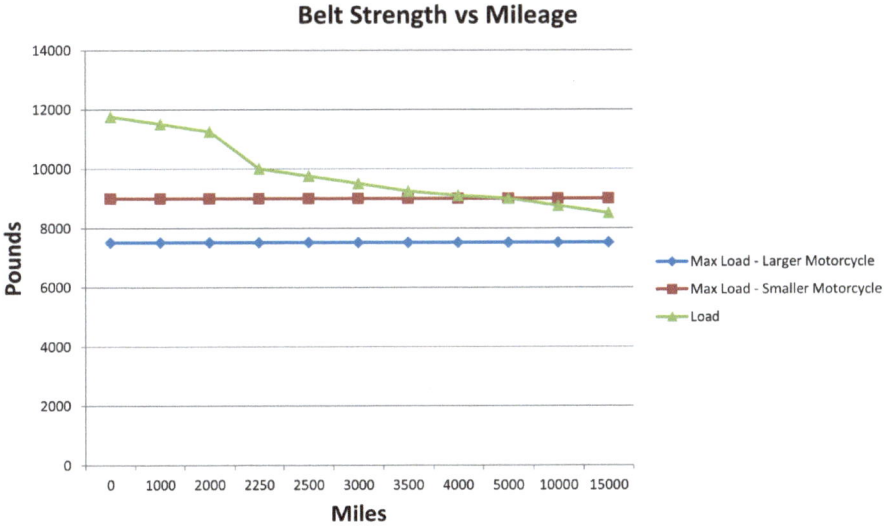

Suddenly, the problem was obvious. Much to everyone's surprise, the smaller motorcycle engine was placing a higher load on the drive belt.

The next step was to create and test some alternative belt designs.

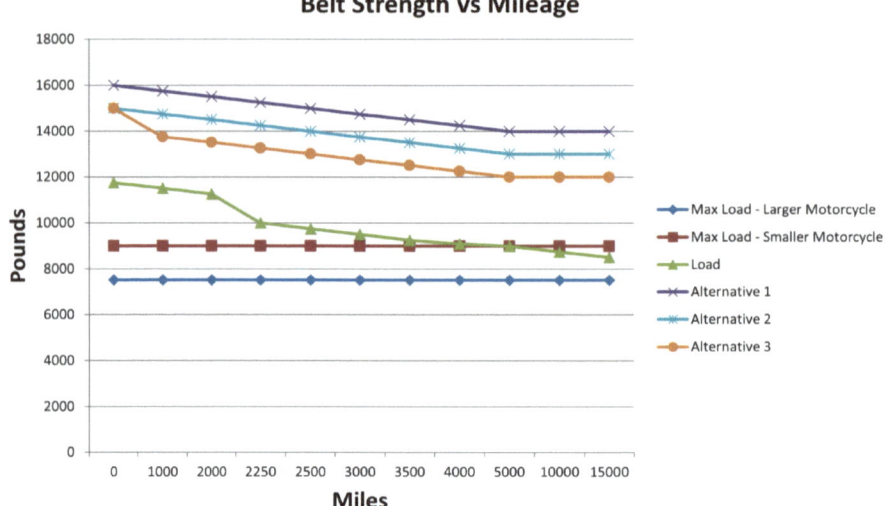

With the limit curves in hand, the team could now select one of the alternative designs with confidence.

Imagine the results in your own organization if you pursued the kind of knowledge development demonstrated by the example above.

Chapter 5 – Converging within the Framework of Scrum

At the place where the roads meet there is no doubt of the convergence.

-   G.K. Chesterton

We have explored the history of the three dominant new product development methods, but the practical question remains: What should we *do*? I propose merging the three within the framework of Scrum.

What is Scrum?

As we learned earlier, Scrum is one of the agile methods. I'm going to give a very brief introduction here. Those interested in learning more can consult a variety of online resources. Here we will use the 100 word definition from Mike Cohen of Mountain Goat Software:

- Scrum is an agile process that allows us to focus on delivering the highest business value in the shortest time.

- It allows us to rapidly and repeatedly inspect actual working systems (software) (every two weeks to one month).

- The business sets the priorities. Teams self-organize to determine the best way to deliver the highest priority features.

- Every two weeks to a month anyone can see a real working system (software) (and decide to release it "as is" or continue to enhance it for another sprint.)

The Sprint structure is the key feature. There is a cadence established by having demonstrations occur every two weeks (or every four weeks depending on your organization). The end of a Sprint provides an opportunity to reflect on what went well and what didn't. These lessons learned can then be applied in the Sprint that is just about to start.

Scrum's "sprint" structure naturally captures some key Lean principles:
1. Flow
2. Pull
3. Perfection
4. Respect for People

Flow
The flow principle is captured by work moving through the system in 30-day increments. These 30-day increments create a natural cadence in an organization. I especially like having demos near the end or beginning of a month.

Pull
Work is pulled through the system by the scheduled demonstrations every 30 days. The team creates the vision and is responsible for doing the work to bring the vision to life. This is true pull, rather than a manager establishing a deadline and pushing a team to meet a schedule created by someone outside the team.

Perfection
Scrum seeks perfection in two ways. The first is the regularly scheduled retrospectives (or reflections) that occur on the 30-day schedule. These meetings are specifically meant to help the team make adjustments to improve their working life. The second mechanism of perfection is Scrum's expectation that work is iterative as well as incremental. The iterative expectation explicitly gives the team permission to refactor earlier work to make it better. Scrum understands that we learn when implementing and this learning is best applied quickly to improve design.

Respect for People
In Scrum, the team determines how much work can be accomplished in the 30-day time period. Work priorities are established outside the team, but the team determines how quickly it can implement the highest priority features.

Chapter 6 – Visual Management

We learn and remember best through pictures, not through written or spoken words.

-   John Medina

A key element in the Toyota way, and Agile development in general, is the use of visual management. Visual management is a way to ensure that organizations remain accountable and transparent. Transparency solves many problems. Have you ever been in an organization that punished the messenger? For example, consider a large project with multiple teams. Perhaps every team is actually behind schedule, but no one wants to be the first team to admit they are behind. The teams end up playing a game to see who will be forced to admit they are behind schedule first. Often, once the first team has made the admission, other teams will come forward and admit being off schedule as well. Nevertheless, the stigma remains with the first team to make the admission. Regardless of who went first, the organization's senior management is caught off guard by the sudden revelation of a schedule slip and usually the magnitude of the slip as well. One of the goals of visual management is to stop the game playing. The team's progress is readily visible and no one needs to be the messenger. The data is on display for all to see. Agile puts the data on display in three ways. The first way we talked about above. It is the sprint demonstration. The second way is the sprint board.

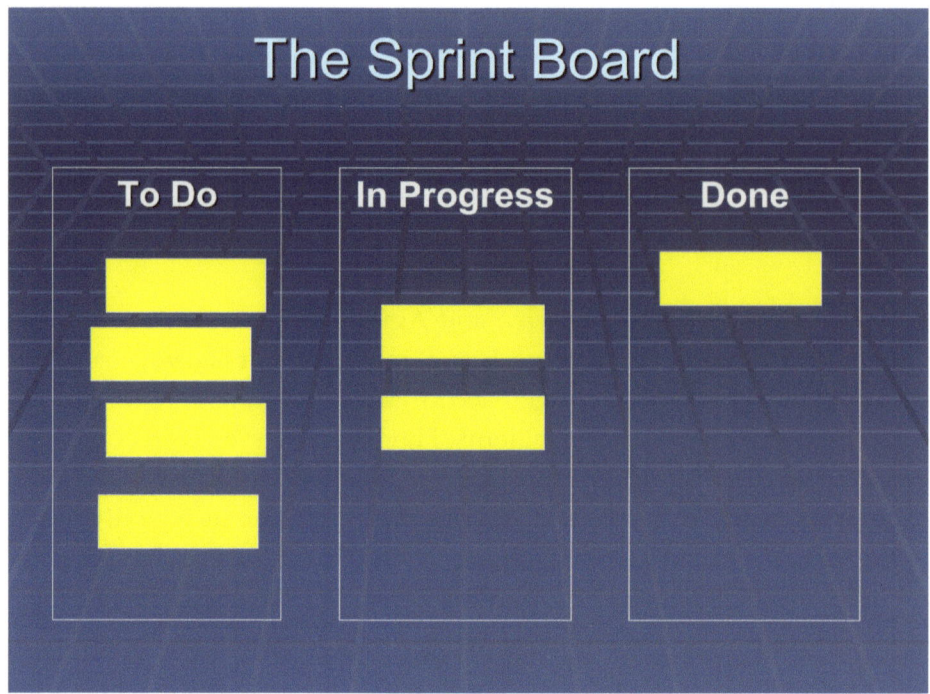

This simple display is easy to maintain and a quick scan of the board, even from six feet away, gives the team and management a measure of progress. An alternative I have found useful is to add "swim lanes" to the board.

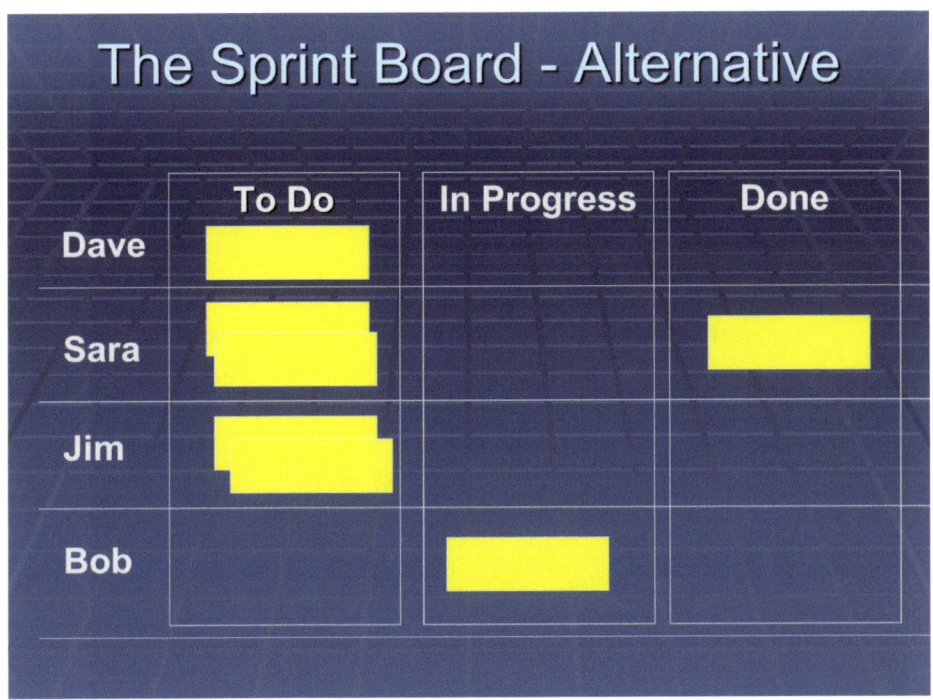

The third way Scrum achieves visual management is with the burn down chart. This is also a simple and easily maintained graph with the same quality of being readable from a distance.

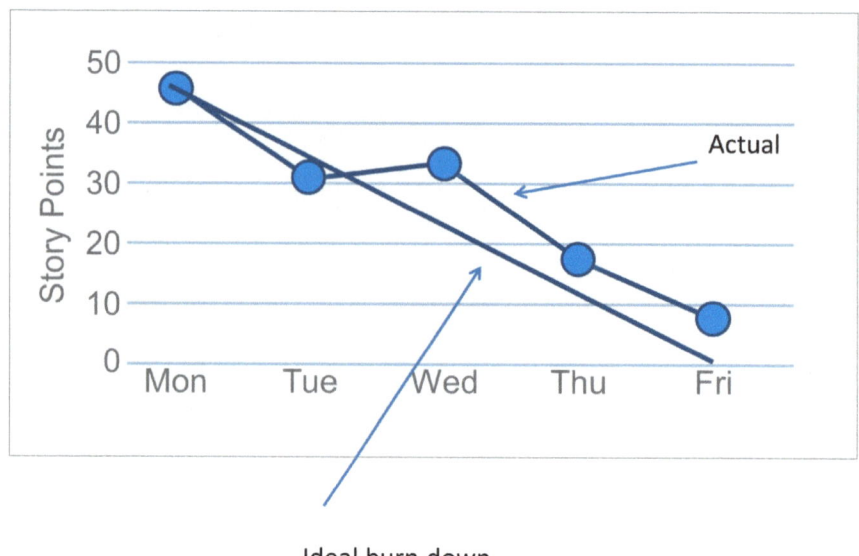

Ideal burn down

A fourth element of visual management, as we discovered above, is the limit curve. The development of limit curves is visible demonstration of what the organization is learning about their product.

Limit curves are more than a method of visual management. They embody the principle that we want to learn about the product we are developing. Out of that knowledge will emerge an ability to create a superior product. Our detailed knowledge will allow us to put systems together in innovative ways and to do so quickly.

Chapter 7 – Five Questions

Using Scrum still leaves us to determine what we should work on first. Scrum would answer simply: "That which has the highest business value." The problem is thinking about what has the highest value for a user may lead us to leave some very important things unanswered. For example, knowing how fast a user wants to do something can be just as important as knowing what the user wants to do. Asking "How fast?" leads to a set of questions such as: What processor should we use? How much RAM and Flash memory do we need? What is a sufficient clock speed?

 I think we must also ask the three questions from knowledge-based development. I would add a fifth question as well: "What do we need to do to remove the highest risk from the project?"

We then have five questions which will help us determine what to do.

The 5 Questions
   1.   What delivers the highest business value?
   2.   What decisions do we need to make?
   3.   What information do we need in order to make those decisions?
   4.   How will we get that information?
   5.   What removes the highest risk elements from the project?

The 5 Questions exist within the context of learning. It is important that we not only make the decisions, but that we systematize our knowledge. We should make the decision knowing how close to the edge we are. We want the creation of the limit curves to be a natural part of how we make a decision and what our information looks like.

Build your schedule as a series of 30-day mini-projects. Each 30-day increment should answer the 5 questions above that remain after the previous increments. Each 30-day increment will conclude with a demonstration of what the development team has accomplished.

Chapter 8 – Living in a Stage-Gate World

If you are employed by a large corporation, it is likely that your projects are conducted with a stage-gate or phase gate process. We need to acknowledge that as a reality and devise a strategy to live within it. Stage-Gates perform an important business strategy as a project portfolio management tool. There will always be more potential projects than there is money to fund them all. Business leaders need a mechanism to keep project progress visible so they can respond to changes in the market or the information obtained during project execution. A typical Stage-Gate process looks like this:

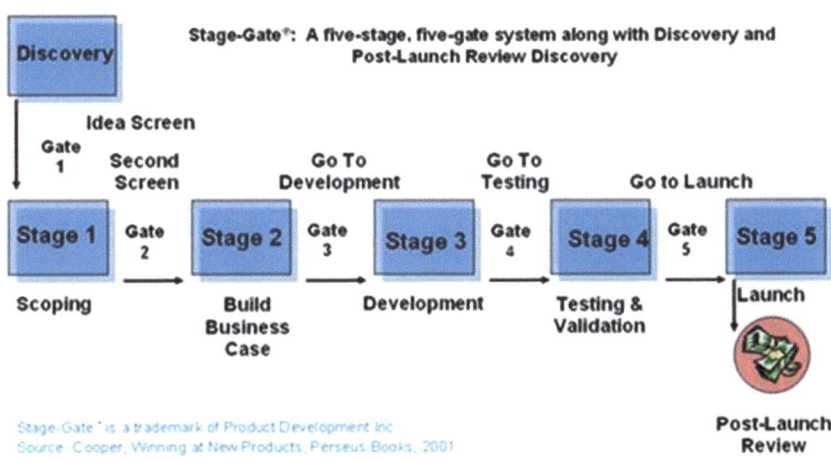

Stage-Gate®: A five-stage, five-gate system along with Discovery and Post-Launch Review Discovery

Discovery

Idea Screen

Gate 1

Second Screen

Go To Development

Go To Testing

Go to Launch

Stage 1 — Gate 2 — Stage 2 — Gate 3 — Stage 3 — Gate 4 — Stage 4 — Gate 5 — Stage 5

Scoping

Build Business Case

Development

Testing & Validation

Launch

Stage-Gate ® is a trademark of Product Development Inc
Source: Cooper, Winning at New Products, Perseus Books, 2001

Post-Launch Review

Look familiar? The stage-gate process was invented by Robert G. Cooper and was first published under that name in 1988. I don't think it is a coincidence stage-gate was developed at the height of the waterfall method's prominence. Stage-gate has exactly the linear structure that waterfall does. In recent years, Robert Cooper has begun to modify the linear approach of Stage-Gate with diagrams such as the one below:

Figure 1: A typical five stage idea-to-Launch *Stage-Gate*® System . The loops are spirals – a series of build-test-feedback-and-revise iterations with the customer

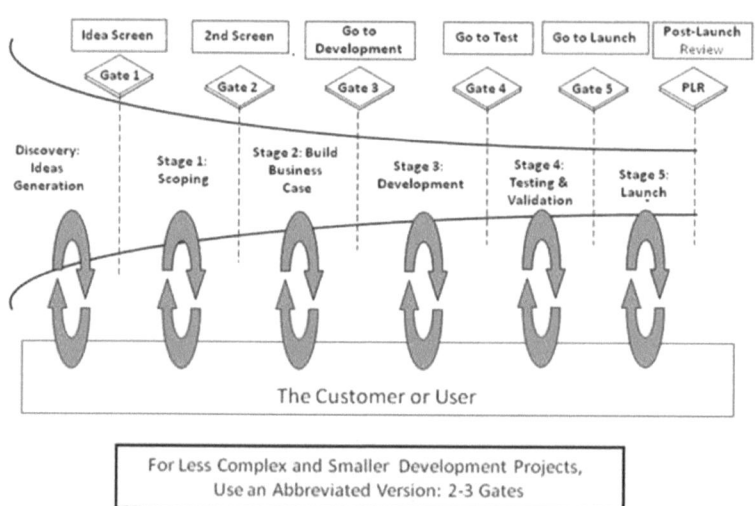

For Less Complex and Smaller Development Projects,
Use an Abbreviated Version: 2-3 Gates

Source: Cooper, endnote 4.

While obviously more agile, I think the diagram misses an important element. See the figure below:

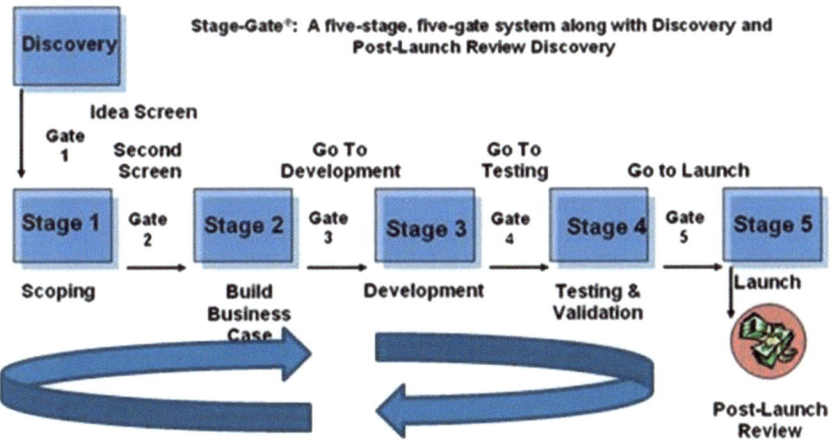

Stage-Gate®: A five-stage, five-gate system along with Discovery and Post-Launch Review Discovery

We want a process that loops through all the phases of the Stage-Gate process. The gating events shouldn't divide Development from Testing & Validation. The gating events should occur after some number of iterations through the entire process. I would suggest writing a project plan that identifies these kinds of loops rather than attempting to modify the corporation's Stage-Gate process. It should be easier to get your project plan approved than to tackle the company's processes directly. Your project will still appear before the gate committee at expected intervals and with visible progress. If you're challenged, you now have the historical background to explain what you are doing and why.

Chapter 9 – Now What?

"Congratulations!
Today is your day.
You're off to Great Places!
You're off and away!"

— Dr. Seuss, *Oh, the Places You'll Go!*

At this point you are a remarkably well equipped traveler in the new product development space. You have learned what the three dominant methodologies are. You have learned some of the history of each. You can see their common traits and what differentiates them. If nothing else, you are now a more knowledgeable and articulate member of your company's staff. What should you *do*? Obviously, I don't know your situation. I can tell you what I did.

1.   Talk about it. Let your voice be heard. Express your desire to improve things. Use the language you have learned.

2.   Act. If you are a team leader, manager, director, etc. implement Scrum. Start doing sprints.

3.   Learn more, and then act. (If you just can't bring yourself to act with what you know, consider hiring a coach.) If you've already started, terrific. Learn what works for you and learn from others.

4.   Repeat steps 1, 2 and 3.

Some would call my plan above "simplistic". Certainly there are entire books written to guide you through implementing change and/or agile at an organizational level. If you would feel better, by all means, read one or more of those books. Do remember, however, nothing will teach you better than trying it.

Above all, your organization must move away from anticipatory development. This doesn't mean run without a plan. It means the most productive organizations have learned and demonstrated the value of adaptive development. The three dominant new product development methodologies share this adaptive mindset. Finally, the economics of new product development have swung decisively in favor of adaptive development as well. It's imperative that your organization beginning adopting these methods.

Chapter 10 – Conclusion

And will you succeed? Yes! You will, indeed! (98 and ¾ percent guaranteed)

— Dr. Seuss, *Oh, the Places You'll Go!*

I hope this concise tour through the dominant new product development methodologies has been informative. My greater hope is that the common threads are now visible. My greatest hope is you will be able to articulate a vision that will tie them together in your organization. At the very least, you should be a more articulate and knowledgeable member at the discussion table as your organization engages in the never ending quest for higher productivity.

Bibliography

[1] I first read Mencken's quote in this context at
http://pascal.gugenberger.net/thoughts/waterfall-accident.html.

[2] http://hbr.org/1986/01/the-new-new-product-development-game/ar/1

[3] http://kenschwaber.wordpress.com/category/kanban/

[4] http://www.slideshare.net/AGILEMinds/michael-kennedy-setbased-decision-making-taming-system-complexity

[5] Learning-First Product Development: An Interview With Michael Kennedy 2009-11-28 — Tobias Fors
http://www.citerus.se/post/220984-learning-first-product-development-an-interview-with

[6] Table from: http://www.slideshare.net/AGILEMinds/michael-kennedy-setbased-decision-making-taming-system-complexity

www.ingramcontent.com/pod-product-compliance
Lightning Source LLC
Chambersburg PA
CBHW041109180526
45172CB00001B/174